The Hot Glue Gun
Chronicles

A Guide to Putting the Pieces Together

A 2023 Philosophy Media Group
Publishing Competition Winning Manuscript

Dr. Ashley Crooks-Allen

Printed in the United States of America
Philosophy Media Group & Kiera Ashlee Talent Co

2024

Editor: Ashlee Haze

Cover Art By: Shay Alexi Stewart-Willis.
Based on an original photograph by Keon Vines.

Table of Contents

Glues You Back Together:
A Foreword from Dr. Amber C. Coleman

Picking Up the Pieces

The thing about hot glue guns is you have to choose to plug them in. And this is exactly what Ashley does. Even when they don't want to, they plug in. Feeling is a choice. Loving is a choice. Mothering is a choice. Embracing your magic is a choice. We can all be feelers. We can all be lovers. We can all be mothers. We can all do magic. I've known Ashley for almost 10 years now, and they never fail to amaze me. How easily they can make words feel like the sway of the breeze. Pierce the veil. Fill the belly like porridge. Water running through your fingers.

As I sit by the pool, I reflect on how through Ashley, I have learned how beautifully complex this world can be. They constantly challenge me to rethink this little thing we are doing called life. To look in the mirror at myself and rethink how my own pieces have come together. To embrace those pieces with love, empathy, and admiration. Being who we are is the fiercest and most radical act of survival and thrive. Being a daughter, being open to diving into the waters of who we have been, who we are, and who we will become (being in our generational memories and stories) is work. Work that an imperialist, capitalist, white supremacist, patriarchal, homophobic world never wants us to do. To tap into our magic. The magic that liberates us to love ourselves and others so freely that we can't tell where one begins and the other ends. "The Hot Glue Gun Chronicles: A Guide to Putting the Pieces Together" is a love letter, a spell, a tribute. Let us feel, let us love, let us magic.

(Re)Arranging New Views

This book is an elegy for the living and the dying. Wherever you may land. As I wrote part of this foreword, I read these poems sitting by the pool. I needed to be near water for this. I noticed as I sat there that I kept catching a reflection of myself. But not me looking back at me. A peripheral reflection. One where I was almost out of reach, I could see part of me and part of the water. The color of the blue pool water was superimposed on my skin, as if I was the water.

What does it mean to be the water? To be what moves, sustains, gives life. Ashley is one of the waters, giving us movement, sustenance, and life with their words, with the oh-so-familiar feelings of being here and there all at once. It is a task to lay oneself bare for others to bear witness. May we all be so brave to bear witness and witness bared.

Glues You Back Together

You can't fight a current. Again, as I sit by the pool reading this text, I am pulled into the current of Ashley's words. Not only being moved by all of the feelings they evoke, but recognizing the currency of what they are saying: what it means to be in our present time and how we cannot escape the path we are collectively on. Through a pandemic, emerging recession, racist/xenophobic onslaught, sexist/homophobic attacks, we are individually and collectively experiencing _____ (insert whatever is on your heart there or the many things we are experiencing). We live in a world where people keep trying to stop the current, thwart systemic change, suppress voices, invisibilize bodies, render our familiar strange. But they can't stop the current. Ashley's words remind me of the importance of the current carrying on, carrying us on.

But, what does it mean to be carried? Ashley reminds me that our stories can carry us. They are full of pain and joy, strategy and truth, challenge and love. Sometimes we need a reminder of the current we're on, to hold fast to where we know the waters can take us: peace, liberation, community. I hope as you read these poems you might follow or join the current. I hope you see a little piece of yourself, your feelings, your dreams, and your desires in Ashley's words. I hope it reminds you of the beloved community you are a part of. I hope it glues you back together.

Author's Note

Daisy's Daughter

Everything that I am is an assemblage of those who came before me. My foremothers Phillis, Daisy, Esmeralda, Trinidad, Mayela poured all of their love into surviving so that I could be here, to write these poems. Isn't survival the most magical manifestation of love? Mothering is the art of unleashing your wildest dreams into the most vulnerable vessel. I see my mothers in every piece of me. This project is a love letter to all of my pieces, every iteration of Ley.

Through this collection, I've found a new appreciation for the fullness of my identity & experiences. In honoring both the light and the dark, we shine the brightest. When we prioritize our connections with each other over the drudge of capitalism, we find our best chance of survival in community. There has to be more out there for us, among the stars. Imaginations ignited; dreams delivered. When we love, we can.

For every other queer AfroLatinx who has spent their entire existence consumed by stories, this book is your sign to free the stories. Let them run wilder than dreams. Truth wash way rumors. Run free. Our rivers run free from sea. We deny destiny manifest. Greed poisons like all the water don't run together, connect, converse. Cross earth, we are sailing our own hearse. Every genocide acts as rehearsal for the next. I expected nothing less. And yet, some still suggest that there is something akin to magic and/or love that make this whole world of wonders worthwhile.

Walk with me while I bear witness to the wild ride we call life.

I've pored over my favorite texts, searching for inspiration of how to preface this experience. I found myself utterly unable to decide what you need to know entering in. You are welcome to come and go as your spirit moves you. It was meant to be heard. Try reading it out loud. Welcome to a colorful collection of stained-glass windows, carefully crafted and curated to contain the contours of creation. I am thrilled to finally share this small piece of me with you.

Love. Light. Liberation.

~ Ley

'Some Yemaya

After Aja Monet's "Unhurt"
/I think I finally put my Finger on Womanhood
/Is This Why They Call it Gender Fluid? Lol
/What is the Opposite of Thirsty?
it's the water!
mm mm mm mm
it is the water
it has always been the water
that tethers us together
flowing through us
across time
the strength of the water bearers before
carrying us through infinity
surviving loveless deserts
damning droughts
turning our search inward
facing ourselves
reckoning with our true power
from ocean to estuaries
reaching out to our sisters
this is how we survive
how we always survive
we are birthed and re-birthed with this water
our depths more memories than mystery
unexplored
beckoning

70
percent
earth/bodies
stories
tides change
hips dip
we carry

on
and on
endlessly
we cry out to
our water goddess
our tempest princess
surrounding me through the deep
I breathe in her tsunami
peace washes over me
swallow
gulp
gasp
quench
drench
it is the water
mm mm mm mm
it was always the water

my first ever research paper was titled
"jean as narrative vessel"
and I am still carrying these stories
my arms are so full
I have reclaimed my own drowning
I call it snorkeling now
deep sea dives
without oxygen
just me and my kin
washed up on the shore
our stories
wrapped up in seaweed
secrets stowed away in the belly of a beast
how do I pay what I owe?
can I barter at least?
I want to be free
but this body is still 70 percent stories
I can't tell
or sell
seashells by the seashore

for my freedom
as the waves swell
I'm reminded
I am
just a vessel
for this
the water

We Should Probably Prepare for the Things We Pray For

today I got good news and I cried
I wish that I could say they were happy tears
I wish I could tell you I sobbed because I was grateful
but I found myself weeping—joy had shown up
and I had no space left for it
I had filled every single crevice of me with grief
I had only today made space for new pain
for even when I finally developed a wary
type of acceptance for depression and anxiety
I discovered withdrawal
frantically feeding my brain like a feral beast
causing me pain when it needs something
but unable to communicate what that something might be
I was so consumed
that a piece of the joy I had been praying for
finally arrived but
it found me unprepared
I had nowhere to put it
I had no idea how to let it in
so I cried
I hope there's space now for the joy
where those tears occupied

Our Five-Foot Giant

knowing my navel cord was buried in your yard
always made me feel safe
I knew my fierce prayer warrior was calling in favors with god
for me
me, your bonita
me, your modela
always yours

lita,
we honor you with our dance
with our laughter
with our love
with our song
though we may be off key
you could always carry a tune

forever the granddaughter of Trinidad
strength like an island
knowledge deep as the ocean
you knew French,
poetry,
proper yard maintenance techniques
the Bible, cover to cover
music
you name it
a truly sophisticated lady

your voice was a song
a siren calling 3 generations of daughters back to you

always back to you
you, the keeper of history and wise words

sankofa begs that we go back to fetch what was left behind
and we will always reach back by
calling your name into our presence
holding your front porch seat
playing your chance numbers
and confidently rocking the biggest sun hats
fan in hand
standing our tallest
on your shoulders
our five-foot giant

How I Wonder What You Are

they call me queen because they see my crown
the way I blend in with my sisters — fellow melanated royalty
my chin always up as I lock eyes with the stars
there is where I see my true self
undefined & shining
a shared type of kinship with the night

#CoronaChallenge/
I Hear Everyone's Doing it

I almost died alone
we were in the midst of a pandemic
so *died* should scare me the most
but it was *alone*
it is *alone*
alone is supposed to keep you safe
but alone is what almost killed me
they say to choose between
6 ft apart or 6 ft under
but what if one just leads to the other

reaching out to people
who've been told to keep a distance
it sounds like a set up to me!
so while everyone is watching the virus
society tries to pick off those of us
unfit for isolation
those deemed unworthy of love
"non-essential" is what I hear
they're calling us these days

so when I needed a hug
and found none
I considered a kiss — from death

#BlackLivesMatter*

when I scream "black lives matter"
there is an asterisk in the back of my throat that whispers
this does not apply to me
my life does not matter
people would barely miss me if I was gone
sometimes I wish that I could take their places
bring back Breonna Taylor or little Aiyana Stanley-Jones
take me instead
maybe I could be more useful as hashtag
I'm sure feeling like a lump hits different from
the inside of a body bag
at least I won't feel like a waste of a toe tag

it's no wonder that I can't breathe
when I consistently feel like a waste of oxygen
why couldn't they take me?
and leave someone here, more deserving
it's unnerving,
the way that I lay in my bed and pray for death
yet, cops have murdered better people in their homes without an
invitation
what I gotta do to get some damn service around here?
they out here protecting and serving my people to death
and yet, they screen *my* calls

Gone Before You Get Here

this is an elegy for pigtails
and clip-on ties
for talking back to your mom
for swinging too high
for sleeping with all of your lights on
for being afraid of the dark
for being afraid to be dark
this is an elegy for black skin.

this elegy isn't really for
Eric Garner
or Michael Brown
or Jordan Davis
or Trayvon Martin
or Renisha McBride.
this elegy is for Aria, due March 17
for Zoe in pre-k
for Marcus entering middle school
for Izzy who should graduate in June
because they have to live
wondering.

we say
if you can just survive
you'll be great
get out of the hood
and into scholastic institutions
with white hoods built into their structures
get you into the suburbs
into bone-straight weaves
into pastels and boat shoes
if only we could get you out of your skin
then you'd be safe

I stand over cradle
my spirit aches
for every accomplishment that finds itself in a grave
before a stage
for building blocks that will form mausoleums
instead of forts
for vases that instead of field-picked Mother's Day daisies
will hold ash
because it seems like every day one of our own falls down.
and they still cannot see that our skin is
drop
dead
gorgeous.
they look at midnight and see shadows instead of stars.
people treat our kids like target practice,
transforming our streets into shooting ranges.
standing their ground
so they can sleep soundly
while children's beds lay empty.

this is an elegy
for all the little black boys and black girls
who either are afraid
or should be.

Trigger Warning

I've heard that I have too much melanin to pop pills and spill my
secrets to strangers
too much strong black woman to take a mental health day
hairy too curly to pull out
and skin too beautiful to scar

so where am I supposed to go when I've had too much?
there's no place for us
I must have forgotten that it could be worse
as if this chemical imbalance is negligible
my people have gotten so much practice forgetting
some days I can barely remember my own name
I settle into caves and plot ways to get voted off this island
drowning seems like a much better exit than a bullet
so many triggers pulled where I'm from that I doubt I could figure
out if it was me that did the deed
just another black body

this here could be a eulogy
today we put to rest
a dearly obscure soul

Ashley was an average girl
of average talent
with average ambition
a girl with brown skin
brown hair
and
brown eyes

though brown is the color of coffee
nobody ever woke up for this brown girl

no amount of Erykah Badu and hot glue could piece me back
together
I love a call from my mom as much as the next girl but sometimes calls
drop
and I'm too tired to pick them back up
I'm too tired to stay strong
too weak to pull a trigger, I'd rather just stop
I've always been afraid of the dark
and somebody keeps turning all of the lights out
bulbs blowing, cracks showing, anxiety growing
keeping my eyes peeled and my heart protected is too much
sometimes
breathing breath is a bit too hard sometimes
but I can't stop because I know they would love to see yet another
black body
one for which nobody can even march in the streets

so where am I supposed to go? I've heard that I have too much
melanin to pop pills and spill my secrets to strangers
too much strong black woman to take a mental health day
hair too curly to pull out
and skin too beautiful to scar

Unbothered

I want to be carefree black girl
tear-free black girl
I want to be gentle
not a danger to myself or others
not wishing I was 6 feet under
I want to be carefree black girl
tear-free black girl
not easily torn
or broken
I want to be waterproof
lifeproof
I need proof that I can do this
that I would be missed
I want to be carefree black girl
tear-free black girl
please love me back world.

#SAYHERNAME

when I heard about #SayHerName,
I immediately wanted to write.
I'm a spoken word artist
this is what I do.

I'm a researcher who studies Black Lives Matter
this is what I do.

I know when we say "Black Lives Matter" people hear "police
brutality against black men"
and not "state sanctioned violence against Black people"
I know Black women are doing the work
that they are founding the movement,
writing love letters that change the world
and that it's so common even among Black women to think that this
movement
that they're doing the work for,
that was founded by them, isn't about them, just men.
this is what I do!

but somehow I did not know what to write.
the men are "missing,"
and the women write them poems
but who writes the poems for the women?
I did not know how to write this poem
there was no template, no draft.

did I write Black women a thank you note?
a love letter?
did I write a call to action on their behalf?
did I write about the grief that hit when I was stopped by the police
and my parents weren't even mad I was speeding
just grateful I didn't end up a hashtag?

so I looked through all my Black Lives Matter poems
and found only bits and pieces here and there
mere whispers of women
I did not know what to do
I did not know what to write
I did not know what to say
so I said her name

Sandra Bland
I probably should've said something when they said she committed
suicide in jail
thinking they could toss Sandy out in the same trash bag they hung
her from

when we both should have been 26,
but instead of seeing her value, they called her collateral damage
Breonna Taylor

when they were still killing our babies in their sleep and walking
away Scott free in 2015
Aiyana Stanley Jones

when they turned our mental illness into a death sentence
Tanisha Anderson

when they came into our homes to serve traffic stop warrants but
left with our sister's life
Korryn Gaines

when they decided that we were living too loud for them so they
stopped you from breathing
Rekia Boyd

When we call them for help, they arrive ready to play a lethal game
of
rock Paper Scissors Shoot!
Charleena Lyle and unborn baby Lyle

what is a name really but a way to call someone into a space?
alive or dead, they are with us
if you've ever been to positive Black girl Instagram
there's a high chance that you've had someone encourage you to
"speak it into existence"
so let's speak them into existence
in this world where there is so little room for us
we must take up as much space as we can

hold Black women a seat at the table
not with your coat or purse
put their name in it to say they are here
to say they matter

I'm sure we've said Black Lives Matter a million times
but do you know who first wrote that love letter to black people?
did you write her a love letter back?
did you address it to
Alicia Garza?

when our organizers were having their homes surrounded by police
calling her a terrorist
did you remember to you call her
Patrisse Cullors?

when my sister was working to ensure that all our people of the
African diaspora knew their lives mattered too, did you remember to
say her name?
Opal Tometi

please
don't just wait until their lives have been stolen
hold them even now before their names
are all we have left to hold

Questions for
My Immigrant Mother

mom, is this the American dream you came here for?
is this what you boarded a plane dressed in your Sunday's best for?
what dad drove a cab in Coney Island for?
left my sister behind for?
mom, how did you come here for a better life?
to a place that doesn't even want us to live?

I never understood how a person could be illegal
but I think we're some of those illegal immigrants that people
consistently complain about
did you know it was illegal to be Black here?
they kill people that look like us here
mom, why would you bring me to a place like this?
some sort of twisted post-birth abortion clinic

I don't think *sana sana* will work on bullet wounds
bush tea won't hide my melanin from them
no matter how much leaf-of-life we bring over
I fear I will die here
and my body will be food for the same trees that they used to lynch
Black bodies
bodies that look just like mine

my navel cord is buried under a mango tree in my grandmother's
yard
and that land is calling out for me
calling me back to safety
I can feel it in my belly bottom
see I know the American flag is the same colors as ours
but this flag here feels like police lights in my rearview mirror
and this American dream is for people who look like us to never see
the light of day

so can we leave now?
mom,
if I promise to learn Spanish and
scrub the floors and
take my cod liver oil every day,
can we go home?
mom
can we please go home?

Home

every day when my dog, Huey and I return to my apartment
I point to the door and say "Home"
I am beginning to suspect that I am trying to teach myself this lesson
as well.

Big Bad

why'd I go and build a home
made of black boys?
such vulnerable creatures
black boys
held together with
prayers duct tape and hope
fragile
existing in the liminal space between life and death
teeter tottering
see them
saw them
them gone
falling apart in my arms
I've been warned
been right here before
on the edge of the burying ground
playing chicken
again
the threats are a game
the fear is real
a carousel of loss
souls not lost
bodies found
black boys

Personally Speaking

since we are not a voiceless people
there is no need for me to speak for all of us
so today, I will just speak for me
when Ami Djaba was stolen from Ghana
& brought to Jamaica
I doubt she ever could have dreamed of me

& yet she, & all of my ancestors
conspired for me to be right here
to be proud
to be Afro-Latinx
to be genderqueer
to be pursuing a PhD
to be pansexual
to be serving my communities
to be me
they did not survive for me to be silent
to stand idle while our people are murdered and disrespected

every day I work on my doctorate
in a building built not just on our people's backs
but on their bodies
when I say that I am standing on the shoulders of giants,
this is not what I wanted it to mean
when I scream about burning shit down
that's looking up at the Ivory Tower
not my hometown
where the Newark riots have already burned everything to the
ground

though I can only speak for me
they keep twisting my words
we are not a voiceless people
so we must speak until they can no longer deny & subvert our
stories
they're always complaining that we're too loud
so let's be loud
let's take up space
in this place where they want us to be silent minorities
supplying their institutional diversity
while they literally bury-
and re-bury our history
under parking lots and graveyards not of our kin

I have to remind them
my Black history is not just body bag and bullet wound
didn't start with slavery and end with Dr. King
is not just marches and court cases
it is so much easier to tell you all of the limits that do not confine
my Black history
because they have tried to keep it so narrow.
but I can start by telling you my Black history is yesterday.
is right this very second that has just passed.
is the very beginning of human life. Is diaspora.
is both front line revolutionary and quiet wallflower.
is not just both. Is always and.
is always present tense.
is grandmothers braiding little girls hair on the porch, veranda,
stoop,
whatever you call it, wherever you're from.

is queer, trans*, and non-binary.
is multiethnic, and multi-racial too.
is not just rapist master but also Loving v. Virginia.
is both first Black woman with a pilot's license and then first
international pilots license, ever.

is both Nigerian and Ghanaian jollof.
is fried catfish and ackee n saltfish.
is AME, the Orishas, the god Ntozake says I can find in myself,
and just "loving herself, as she loves others".
is Malcolm X. Is Afro-LatinX.
is step and Black *Queer Theory: A Critical Anthology.*
is Whitney as the fairy godmother to Brandy's Cinderella.

is the prayers to present pipeline.
is cosplaying as The Black Panther. Is the Black Panthers.
is riot and lunch counter sit-in.
is back of the bus and front of the classroom.
is #BlackLivesMatter, #SayHerName, and #BlackTwitter.
is perm, 'fro, locs, crochet, sew-in, twist-out, tucked under a hijab,
or whatever the hell else I want depending on the day, or mood.

it is stolen and found.
it is AAVE and Xhosa and Igbo and Creole and Gullah.
it is continental and diasporic.
but most importantly it is not just mine
it is ours.

Cesarean

there are parts of me
I cannot touch and there are
parts I cannot feel

Surrender

I prayed for a baby
but of course
I would give birth to a metaphor

for the brightest star in our seemingly endless night
for the sun in our gray skies
shining light where we couldn't see
for my son
born three in the morning

my son is my morning
my reason to wake up
the little voice in my spirit that says
"keep going"
belongs to him

I have yet to hear his voice
I have yet to hear him laugh
but his joy speaks volumes
he is the torch that lights my path

he is a metaphor for
a sunrise
a smile
a science experiment
a song

I could go on and on
I thought I just asked for a baby

but my son came with stars and the moon
tiny explosions
a new point of view
each day

even with constellations painted across EEG scans
he's a daily reminder that "I can."
even when I don't quite understand

he reigns
over my heart and mind
royal bloodlines
and a fresh outlook on life
every time he opens his eyes
he reminds me what it means to be alive

when I prayed for a baby
god gave me more
than I could have ever asked for
with faith in my way maker
pushing me past pain
I didn't think I could endure
limitless potential
a perfect metaphor

Front Porch Epistemology

the academy doesn't trust me
nor I it
I trust people
my people
to be experts in their own lives
those that approach Black and Brown people with distrust
are the ones who hit you with the
"I could not have imagined…[insert blatant insidious racist truth]"
what if we could imagine
ancient for some
and yet also brand new
hearing the truth from our different ways of knowing
I imagine
we-search
trusting our co-conspirators
we know what anti-Black feels like
we have stared it in the eye
and stood tall with its stank breath in our face
yet you want to question the validity of our reality
because it's not in your textbook
not in a journal
reviewed by whose peers?
not mine!
how many Black fingers pointing out racism until you believe them
black testimony still only 3/5 as loud
as though knowledge is only that
once it's written down
mother tongue
washed away
oral tradition survives
you can keep your gates
our work is in connecting lives

Soft

seeing stormy shores
saw sinking sun/ sis shifted
siempre she survives

Can of Snakes

This poem has a trigger warning for self-harm & sexual assault or rape, I never say rape./ Go on and leave the room if you like/ I would leave the room if I could/ I swear I must have left the room that night/ How else do our so-called friends, brothers, lovers enter my house uninvited?/ He swears he didn't take anything/ I swear he didn't take anything/ But now I have an alarm that seems to go off randomly/ And a guard dog that barks at me/ I don't think it even knows whose house this is/ I don't know that I know whose house this is/ I keep trying to fill it with new things that say/ This is mine/ This can here is mine cans last forever. That is the point. I can open it when I want to./ I do this on my own terms like I didn't get to then./ This is where it gets tricky, I've decided to open the can of worms now./ I flipped the can's tab but peeling the metal back is excruciating./ I do not tell Dr. Leach how I first met D when I was seventeen./ I was neon skirt looking for the party/ and he was Bill Cosby sweater/ knowing exactly where the party was./ He was charming./ He liked lasagna./ I never had to sleep alone for the first month of college./ You could catch us any given weekend in our room./ It was his room but it was really ours. /Our room was the place for parties./ My phone was the strobe light./ I always had a dance partner/ and someone to take another shot with.

I learned in my philosophy of literature class about the form./ It was like a template from which all things came./All chairs were modeled after the form of the chair./ I thought D was the form of the beautiful./ I never told Dr. Leach how I would watch him sleep./ The outside lights would peak through the blinds,/ keeping me up to marvel at his beautiful silhouette./ He said our relationship was unhealthy/ I wasn't really sure/ what about our love was unhealthy./ He loved me back, he just wasn't ready yet./ I went back to my room./ I broke a pencil sharpener/ just to get my hands on a blade / just to get a blade on my wrist./ Now this was unhealthy.

I thought I just canned what happened but it was all of him./ Every single piece of him was in this can./ Watching my favorite fraternity unveil their new line./ I stood on tiptoe to catch/ glimpses of the crimson & creme/ until I realized he was one of them./ Later, he'd tell me he'd gotten better at a lot of things since he became a kappa./ You could always spot him with his cane over one shoulder or the other./ He used to be a page in my journal that I always skipped, so how did he become a tightly sealed can buried deep beneath the earth?

Nothing was weird when he came to my dorm./ I was staying in Turman hall, where he lived freshman year-/ where I lived for the first month of my freshmen year./ Things were full circle now./ We were older, more mature, friendly even./ We had a few drinks because sometimes you just gotta turn up on a Wednesday,/ (his sentiments, not mine.)/ But it was summer, so why not?/ We got to talking about how things have changed/ and he said, "I've gotten better at a lot of things since I became a Kappa."/ I asked, "like what?"/ And he said, "like sex. You should let me prove it to you."/ I declined/ I tried to get back to less awkward ground./ It worked and we were back to the casual chatter that opens doors for/ someone's exit. Then he suggested more shots./ I thought I'd had enough, but what's another shot or two between friends?/ "You should let me prove it to you," he said again/ and this time I said/ "sure"/ Not the enthusiastic yes /that had come out of my sober eighteen-year-old mouth/years before

/ but "sure"
/ "sure" is for "would you like fries with that?"
/ A drunk "sure" is /not an enthusiastic yes.
/ "Sure" does not mean take my clothes off or do with me what you will.
/ I did not tell Dr. Leach how easy it is to climb inside me/ if you give me a few shots and pressure me into "sure."

I was definitely not sure/
I woke up very unsure
and alone/

I was just one of those girls now,/ the ones who get drunk and make bad decisions./ Nothing had happened to me./ See? I told you/ nothing had been stolen./ This wasn't anything out of the ordinary./ Sex was one of the first things in my life I could control/ I could give my body, freely.

/I had given myself to him before/ I danced naked with him,/ blasting Lonely island's "I Just Had Sex" so the whole hall could hear./ I used to be proud./ This was just like freshman year/except I can't really remember/ but if I can't remember then it couldn't have been that bad/ Right?

I started packing it up then./All of it/ except for the emptiness./ Nothing had happened worth talking about./ Every memory packed tightly into the can./ Every single utterance of "you should let me prove it to you" was packed./ I told Dr. Leach I had everything under control./ I am not sure that I have everything under control./ I decided to open the can now because I'm tired of it resurfacing unannounced./ That can had entirely too much power over me and now I am done./This is what I didn't tell Dr. Leach/ this isn't even everything./ Still, this was where the tears came from this summer/ when I said, "I don't want to do this anymore"/and J said, "I'm almost done."/ This is me standing up for myself. This is my enthusiastic "no." This is where I stop feeling like people are entitled to my body./This is where all my power is./ In this empty can/ one I am afraid to pick up because the edges are still so sharp.

If You Are Called to Identify My Body

my sex bracelets are permanent
the flesh colored ones means I'm down for anything
always down for everything
I am always down
shoulders down
head down
eyes down
cast me aside when I am used up
or you are done
whichever comes first
I've got new wounds to tend to
burns to soothe
stitches to sew
just let me know when you are done

my sex bracelets are permanent
I'm so thin
there's barely room for any more of them to fit on my wrists
I let them fill me to the brim
with anything you can imagine
I'm just so empty
so full of bad ideas and one night stands
I can't even let them hold my hand
because then they might see that

my sex bracelets are permanent
and no amount of shea and wishing them away will work
they are scar and wound
and the one set of holes I won't let them get into
these bracelets are one way exits
in case of emergency and sometimes red
I invite them inside and then play dead

my body is a murder mystery
a crime scene
I've got no forms of ID on me
but my sex bracelets are permanent

Private Lessons

when will she learn
that going from
keeping her mouth shut
to keeping her mouth full
won't help her find her voice?
that getting down on her knees
to do anything but pray
won't bring her any closer to God?
that disrespecting herself won't earn her respect from others?
that she's better than that?

I wonder if her eyes are too much sun to see
that he doesn't love her
at least not the way he ought to
still she swears she hears 'I love you's in his moans
when she does it just the way
he taught her

it's almost as though she thinks she is stuck inside of a man
and she can somehow suck herself out
like he can inject her with everything she's missing
and she doesn't have to worry
because his too smooth voice promised her
"it'll only hurt for a minute"
pretty sure girl's got hymens confused with promises
as what were meant to be
broken

she keeps her legs open
flickering neon sign across her face
no words have to be spoken
she is the perfect play thing
a doll with cracked porcelain
and holes in all the right places

you can insert yourself wherever you'd like
just be sure to be quick
she can't stay for the night
that's the kind of thing you do
when you love someone
the way you ought to

plus of course she needs time to
find her way home
she can't remember
what her mom taught her
sometimes she forgets
she's even somebody's daughter
as if someone would even want to
call her their own

she gets home
crawls into bed alone and cries
she doesn't even realize
she makes the sun rise

I get home crawl into bed alone
and I cry
I don't even realize
I make the sun rise

when will I learn
that going from keeping my mouth shut
to keeping my mouth full
won't help me find my voice?
that getting down on my knees
to do anything but pray
won't bring me any closer to God?

Astro-not

"good morning class.
who wants to tell us what they want to be when they grow up?"

"oo oo pick me!
I want to be an astronaut!"

guess Mrs. W figured she didn't have to ask
what he was going to be instead
probably already had it in her head
that she'd get the answer
I would get when I asked what he was doing
any time of any day
it was always the same
"nothing"

my best friend wanted to be an astronaut
so why is his daily high the closest to the moon I've ever seen him
get?
sure, making him show up to school the day we learned stars
are just balls of hot gas is something I regret
but only because it seems like he made it his goal
to create a solar system in his basement ever since
everyday
he'd light up
fill the room with warm clouds
and wait to see stars
but his daily high isn't what disturbed my mind
it was the landings
the crash landings into a state of hopelessness left just for him

he'd get the munchies
and eat up whatever hope he had left
when he couldn't find any more
he'd eat up whatever hope I had for him
I was really hoping
he could've made it to outer space
out of this place
where if he wasn't asking "paper or plastic"
his only other choices were to be in a cage or in that box
only remembered on t-shirts and tweets once a year
everybody has already forgotten about the air-locked doors that
kept him from graduation
memories have faded
and now he's nothing but his locked hair
he'd always ask
"why establish a career when you know you'll be gone in just a few
years?"
and I couldn't argue with that
still I tried once last month to remind him of his dream
but he just said "nah son. don't know nothin bout no NASA"
sounded to me like words straight out the mouth of master
I mean mister
Mr. R
should have made sure he knew physics
but just like all the rest of the alphabet soup of teachers
he started acting like he was psychic
like he knew dreads wouldn't show up for class
or pass his exams
or get a diploma
Mr. R should've tried harder
my best friend didn't fail school
school failed him

he's just one of the half of the 40,000
that got his moon rock collection swapped for rocks of a less alien
kind
just the half of the 40,000

that we're allowed to view that rolled up piece of paper as just more
rolling paper
just the half of the 40,000
that couldn't put textbooks before texting on their own
just the half of the 40,000
Newark public school soldiers who could not survive the falling
grenades of school with failing grades

just the half of the 40,000. . .

when even your teachers don't expect you to get your diploma
you might as well sit home
and make solar systems in your basement
fill the room with warm clouds
and wait till you see stars

please forget you ever wanted to be an "astro-not"
I've seen how they teach you to do that
when you get your chance
you tell them
"I want to be an 'astro-can'"
"I want to be an 'astro-will'"
tell them "teach me how
I need to be an 'astro-are'"

Cosmos I: Stargazer

he's always too busy looking up
looking out
light years ahead of his time
of this time
what could be our time

he can't see right beside him
and I get it
somewhere out there
are our future selves
our better selves
a perfect moment

but what if we're just obsessed with the shadows of stars already
done?
what if we were looking at opportunities already come and gone
there was a time when I could have just moved on
but it kind of came and went

and I know you'd prefer to look at something beautiful like the stars
but would you mind
if I
watched with you?

Gate 17 Symphony

excuse me!
excuse me sir,
I think you might be my father
I haven't seen him in a while
but your silence sounds the same

your frown lines are the exact same place his were
I don't think he ever learned how to smile
much less laugh
probably because laughter sounds a bit like music
poetry sounds like music
love sounds like music
he never did too much care for music

you don't look like you care much for music either
or anything at all for that matter
not even me
I'm pretty sure you're my father now

tell me about yourself
well at least answer my questions
tell me, do you hate sleeping?
wait better yet
tell me do you hate dreaming?
I forgot you have to care to hate

I know this is a stretch
but please tell me you remember
that beautiful little gapped tooth girl with pigtails
no?
well she has been patiently waiting the entire time you've been
gone
I gave her her first hug in years and told her you'd be back soon
but I can only lie for so long

I won't do your dirty work for you
you tell her your secret
tell her you're an addict
addicted to not being a father
addicted to being everywhere but where she is

tell her how you love to get high
how you love the paper cuts from boarding passes that read:
Newark Liberty International to:
Costa Rica, Panama, Spain, Puerto Rico, Jamaica, Colorado,
Florida, Vegas
everywhere but where you belong

tell her how you love the roar of jet engines more than the sound
of her voice
probably because her voice sounds a little too much like music
tell her how you'd rather hear her cry because it sounds a little less
like music
her voice sounds like pure poetry but that's way too close to music
her voice is pure love
and some say that love is synonymous with music
but you never did too much care for music
right?
yeah
you are my father.

Father's Day

father,
how did you watch your only son suffer?
how did you survive the heartbreak of
gifting your beloved child to this cruel world?
can you teach us how to bear witness?
even when the misery feels too much to bear
the tears in my son's eyes flow from mine, too
you know what that's like
don't you?
when Jesus wept,
did you?

Somebody's Mother

before I was your mother,
I used to be somebody.

somebody brilliant
somebody captivating
somebody creative
and talented
and quirky
somebody special.

I didn't have it all figured out of course.
but I did have something.
I had a smile that could light up a room.
I had a laugh that could not be contained.
I had a face that told all truth all times.
I had vision
and drive.
and a way with words.

so when my grandmother passed away and
someone who loved her like she was her own mother said,
"she gave all of her to us that she could"
I thought wow,
to be loved like that is so rare.
that is something special.
to give all that you have.

so I gave you my smile.
I gave you my brilliance.
I gave you my creativity.
and I gave
and I gave.

and I found I always had enough to give to myself too.

so yes.
I used to be somebody,
used to have something.
now I've got more than I ever had before.

when your heart is full, you have enough to share.
so I gave.
I gave you the world.
and gave the world, you.

Side Quests

what am I doing?
searching for lost poems
chasing after what-ifs
reaching back for a time long gone
pulling back empty fists
finding hole after hole
where is it?

.

www.ingramcontent.com/pod-product-compliance
Lightning Source LLC
LaVergne TN
LVHW051430080426
835508LV00022B/3330